MIAMI DOLPHINS · SUPER BOWL CHAMPIONS

VII, JANUARY 14, 1973
14-7 VERSUS WASHINGTON REDSKINS

VIII, JANUARY 13, 1974
24-7 VERSUS MINNESOTA VIKINGS

SUPER BOWL CHAMPIONS

MIAMI DOLPHINS

AARON FRISCH

LEWIS CROZER LIBRARY CATION
CHESTER, PA 19013

COVER: RUNNING BACK LARRY CSONKA

PAGE 2: RUNNING BACK PATRICK COBBS CELEBRATING A
TOUCHDOWN

RIGHT: RUNNING BACK RICKY WILLIAMS ESCAPING A
TACKLER

Published by Creative Education
P.O. Box 227, Mankato, Minnesota 56002
Creative Education is an imprint of The Creative Company
www.thecreativecompany.us

Book and cover design by Blue Design (www.bluedes.com)
Art direction by Rita Marshall
Printed by Corporate Graphics in the United States of
America

Photographs by Corbis (Atlantide Phototravel), Dreamstime
(Rosco), Getty Images (Doug Benc, Focus On Sport, George
Gojkovich, Sam Greenwood, Walter Iooss Jr./Sports
Illustrated, Kidwiler Collection/Diamond Images, Takashi
Makita/NFL, Ronald Martinez, Al Messerschmidt/NFL,
Ronald C. Modra/Sports Imagery, JC Ridley/NFL, George
Rose, Rhona Wise/AFP)

Library of Congress Cataloging-in-Publication Data

Frisch, Aaron.
Miami Dolphins / by Aaron Frisch.
p. cm. — (Super Bowl champions)
Includes index.
Summary: An elementary look at the Miami Dolphins
professional football team, including its formation in 1966,
most memorable players, Super Bowl championships, and
stars of today.
ISBN 978-1-60818-021-9
1. Miami Dolphins (Football team)—History—Juvenile
literature. I. Title. II. Series.

GV956.M47F75 2011
796.332'6409759381—dc22   2009053505

CPSIA: 040110 PO1141

First Edition
9 8 7 6 5 4 3 2 1

CONTENTS

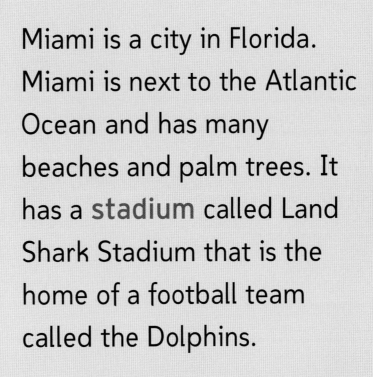

SUPER BOWL CHAMPIONS

Miami is a city in Florida. Miami is next to the Atlantic Ocean and has many beaches and palm trees. It has a **stadium** called Land Shark Stadium that is the home of a football team called the Dolphins.

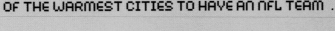

... MIAMI IS ONE OF THE WARMEST CITIES TO HAVE AN NFL TEAM ...

7

DOLPHINS FACTS

First season:
1966

Conference/division:
American Football Conference, East Division

Super Bowl championships:
VII, January 14, 1973
14–7 versus Washington Redskins

VIII, January 13, 1974
24–7 versus Minnesota Vikings

Training camp location:
Davie, Florida

NFL Web site for kids:
http://nflrush.com

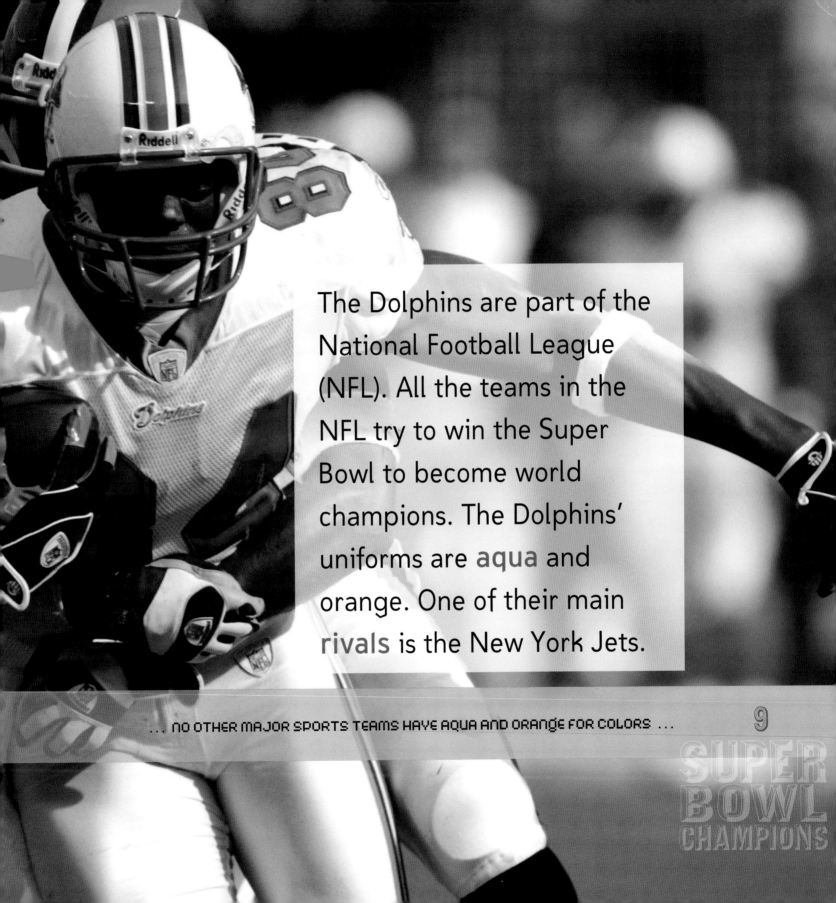

The Dolphins are part of the National Football League (NFL). All the teams in the NFL try to win the Super Bowl to become world champions. The Dolphins' uniforms are **aqua** and orange. One of their main **rivals** is the New York Jets.

SUPER BOWL CHAMPIONS

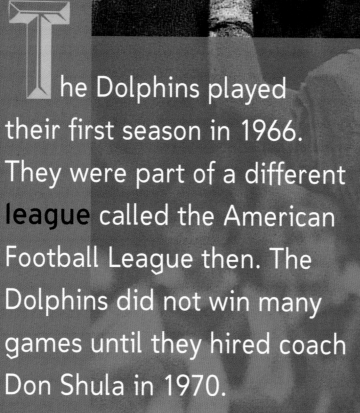

The Dolphins played their first season in 1966. They were part of a different **league** called the American Football League then. The Dolphins did not win many games until they hired coach Don Shula in 1970.

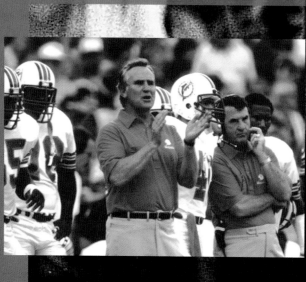

... DON SHULA (LEFT) AND DOLPHINS PLAYERS IN A MUDDY GAME (RIGHT) ...

11

SUPER
BOWL
CHAMPIONS

MIAMI DOLPHINS

Quarterback Bob Griese helped make the Dolphins much better, too. They won Super Bowls VII (7) and VIII (8) after the 1972 and 1973 seasons. In 1972, they did not lose any games! No other NFL team has ever done that.

12

Say It Like This

Griese:
GREE-see

In 1983, the Dolphins got a new quarterback named Dan Marino. The next season, he threw 48 touchdown passes and helped Miami get to the Super Bowl. But this time, the Dolphins lost.

SUPER BOWL CHAMPIONS

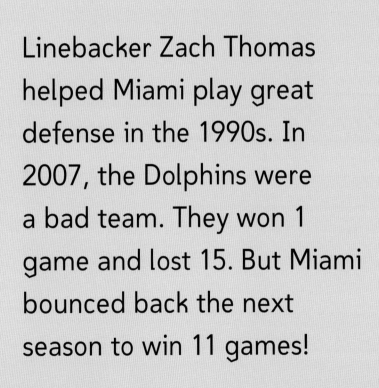

Linebacker Zach Thomas helped Miami play great defense in the 1990s. In 2007, the Dolphins were a bad team. They won 1 game and lost 15. But Miami bounced back the next season to win 11 games!

... ZACH THOMAS LED THE DOLPHINS IN TACKLES FOR 10 SEASONS ...

15

Two of the Dolphins' first stars were Larry Csonka and Nick Buoniconti. Csonka was a powerful running back. Fans called him "Zonk." Buoniconti was a tough linebacker who was the captain of the defense.

... NICK BUONICONTI (NUMBER 85) WAS SHORT, BUT HE WAS STRONG ...

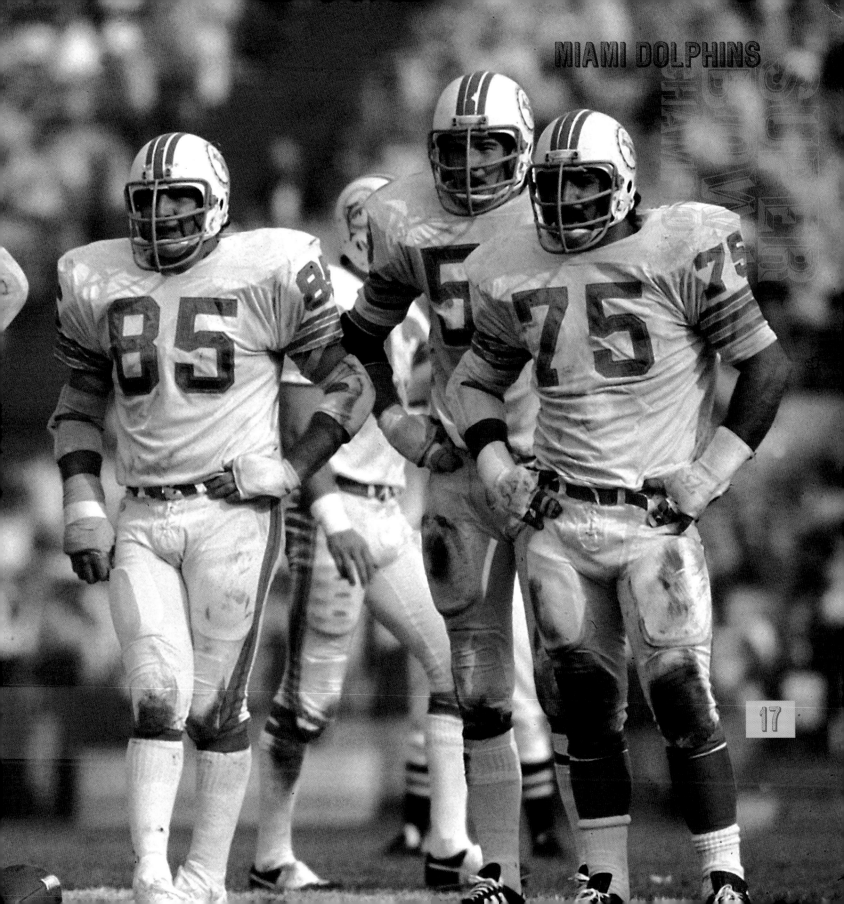

17

WHY ARE THEY CALLED THE DOLPHINS?

Miami is next to the Atlantic Ocean. There are many dolphins in the ocean near Miami. Dolphins are animals that can swim fast and are very smart.

SUPER BOWL CHAMPIONS

Wide receiver Mark Clayton joined Miami in 1983. He caught many passes from Dan Marino. Fast defensive end Jason Taylor was another Dolphins star. In 2006, he won an award as the NFL's best defensive player.

... MARK CLAYTON SCORED 82 TOUCHDOWNS PLAYING FOR THE DOLPHINS ...

19

SUPER BOWL CHAMPIONS

The Dolphins added new offensive tackle Jake Long in 2008. He was a powerful blocker. Miami fans hoped that he would help lead the Dolphins to their third Super Bowl championship!

... JAKE LONG WAS A 6-FOOT-7 LINEMAN WHO WEIGHED 315 POUNDS ...

GLOSSARY

aqua — a color that is greenish blue, like seawater

captain — the leader of a group

league — a group of teams that all play against each other

rivals — teams that play extra hard against each other

stadium — a large building that has a sports field and many seats for fans

23

INDEX

WITHDRAWAL